# First My Mother, Forever My Friend

## COLORING BOOK

### JESSICA MAZURKIEWICZ

My mom helped me to be all that I am.

DOVER PUBLICATIONS, INC.
MINEOLA, NEW YORK

*Thank you, Mom, for teaching me the importance of loving what I do and the joy of a cozy home and a happy heart!*

*Thanks also to my creative assistant, Jen O'Donnell.*

*—Jess*

Sweet and sometimes humorous sayings accompany many of the drawings in this lovely collection of 31 designs celebrating mothers. From the sentimental "A mom's hug lasts long after she lets go" to the amusing "If you love your mother, let her sleep," these delightful images will be sure to bring your own mother to mind. Intended for the advanced colorist, the pages feature backgrounds that include flowers, candles, baking items, jewelry, and luscious desserts. The illustrations in this book are printed on one side only and are perforated for easy removal and display.

*Copyright*

Copyright © 2019 by Dover Publications, Inc.
All rights reserved.

*Bibliographical Note*

*First My Mother, Forever My Friend Coloring Book* is a new work, first published by Dover Publications, Inc., in 2019.

*International Standard Book Number*

*ISBN-13: 978-0-486-82669-1*
*ISBN-10: 0-486-82669-4*

Manufactured in the United States by LSC Communications
82669401    2018
www.doverpublications.com

Sometimes when I open my mouth, my mother comes out.

Mom Okaasan
Matka
Ma MOTHER
MAMI
Mère Mamá
MAJI Mater
MOER
Máthair
Madre MUTER

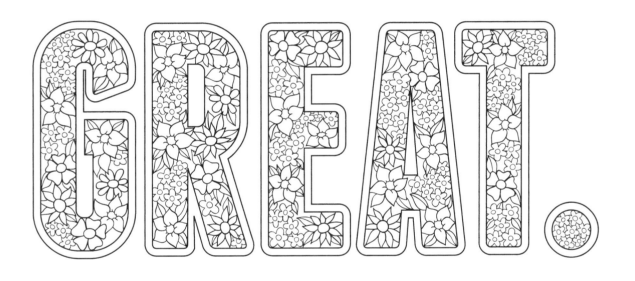

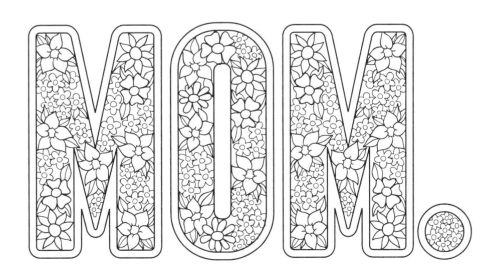

**mother**

(muh*th*-er) - noun

One person who does the
work of ten for free.

HOME

is where
your
Mom is

A MOM'S HUG

LASTS LONG AFTER
SHE LETS GO.

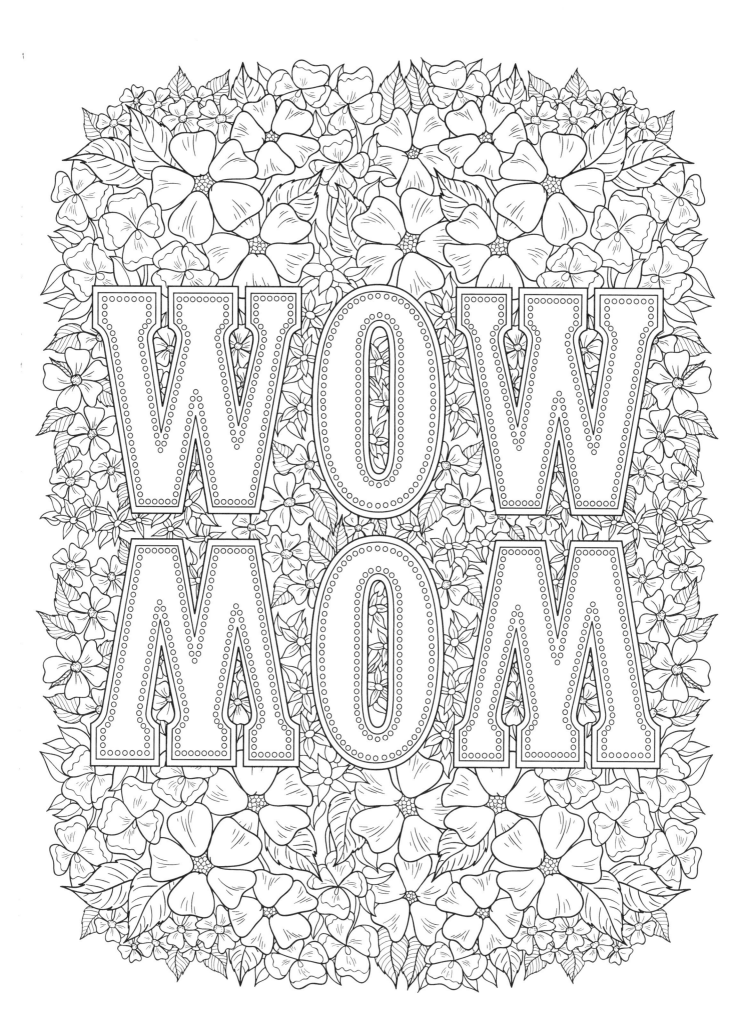

My mom knows what you did... and she doesn't like you!

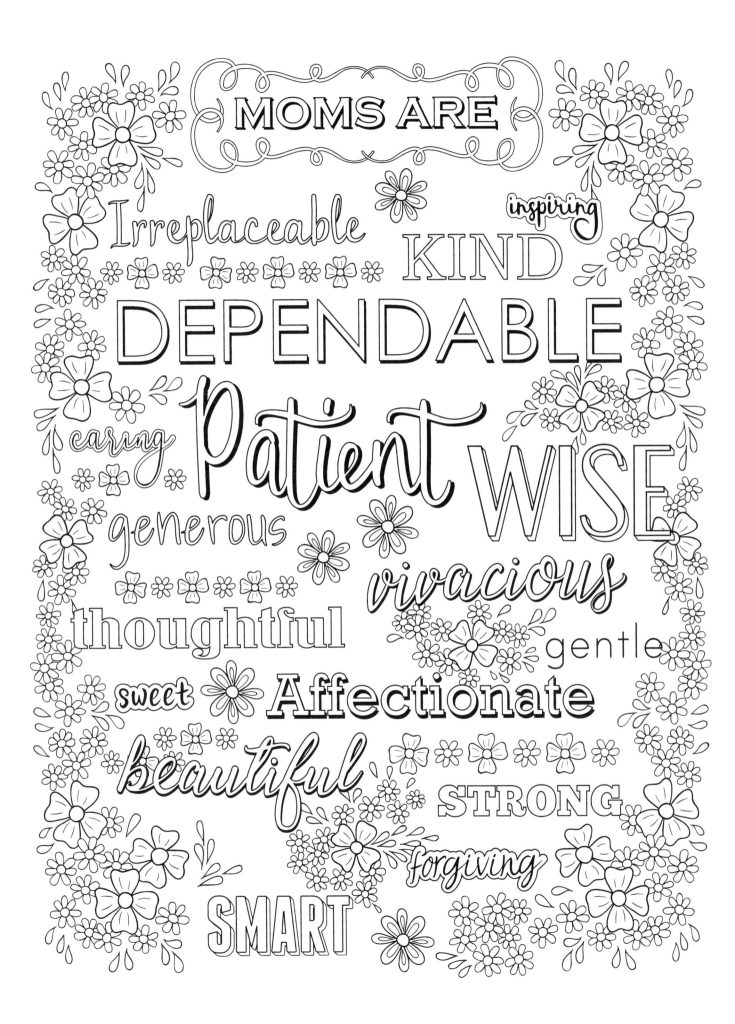

Always my
Mom
Forever my
Friend